calling in black

nicholle ramsey

TALKING DRUM

Seattle, Washington

Paperback 978-1-7360746-1-9
Kindle 978-1-7360746-2-6
EPUB 978-1-7360746-3-3

Library of Congress Cataloging Number on file with the publisher.

Cover illustration by Ejiwa "Edge" Ebenebe
Interior illustrations by Lukas Ramsey
Publishing and Production by Concierge Publishing Services

Printed in the United States of America
10 9 8 7 6 5 4 3 2 1

This collection of poetry is dedicated to those loved ones who believed in me and inspired me to keep moving forward.

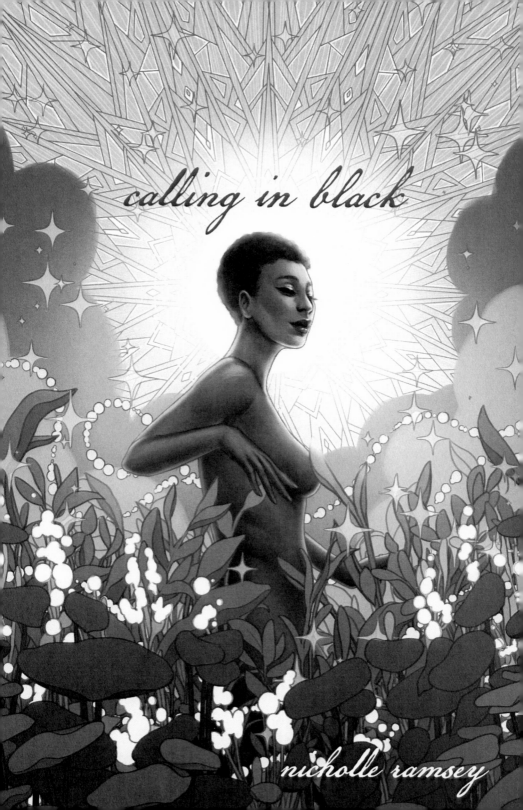

calling in black

nicholle ramsey

author's note

the book *calling in black* is a series of confessions and stories by nicholle ramsey. it is inspired by the sunniest day in february, the way your stomach feels on a roller coaster, and the moldy orange that ruins the bunch all wrapped into one collection. *calling in black* is a reclamation of tears and body. it is an ardent need to desire and care for self and the community we are surrounded by.

sometimes

sometimes i sit on the bathtub floor,
naked, of course, let water run hot.
hit my face like an imitation drowning
or *elsewhere* rebirth. sometimes
i trace the spines of books as if i know
their whole story, superficial,
but sometimes the spine tells all
like a book read over and over again
his snakes, cowers, and curls. collapsible.
as if he is my copy of *the little prince*,
picking it up even though i know the ending.
sometimes i call because it's all my fingers
know to do. and we shoot shit. but sometimes
i call because sleepy dream soles
float down river, pinch me, please,
until i open my eyes again,
because sometimes i like to stare
into your eyes at sunrise. the warmth
of getting lost in green comforts,
but i am forgetting the whole forest
is behind you.
i hold your body by the roots, i pine.
and sometimes i run away to the back waters
of mississippi with only a pack of cigarettes,
let my toes prune in the river
while i chain smoke until i am ready to go home.
sometimes i think you are my home,
my naïve childhood game of make believe,
my white picket fence, garden, loveseat,
weird art in the living room. my permanent.
and sometimes you have to wake me up, remind me
that you are not even my cardboard box
not for always, just sometimes.

tastes of mania

my manic tastes like injera
made with cabbage and lamb fresh
from the homeland
as i research the price of plane tickets
i hear ethiopia is beautiful this time of year
my manic tastes like half read books and skipped therapy sessions
like dancing too close to beach bonfires burning soles
like a ten mile bike ride after i say i am tired
my manic tastes like two am art creations and over sharing
like rum and coke with so much rum that you cannot taste the coke
like stardust wishes dizzy from spinning circles between sleeping
tomatoes
like peeing on school buildings and over cleaning bathrooms
my manic tastes like semen
like mac and cheese and skinny dipping
like confessions and reconciliation
but none of that religious shit
my manic tastes like shoplifting wine-named lipsticks
and spin the bottle watermelon kisses
like *i know we just met but i think i love you*
do you want to go to my best friend's wedding with me
my manic tastes like an entire package of oreos and a 1.9 lb bag of
swedish fish
like the doctor's appointment where the nurse practitioner
asked me if i knew how to perform safe sex
and i told her if she was as stoned as me
she would have also forgotten a condom
my manic is a stoner gazing in front fully stocked pantry
trying to cram all of life between these lips
before the looming depression hits.
depression tastes like mothballs.
and my mother's potato salad.
cold. bland.
so my manic is gonna eat while it can while i can

roots

the horseradish peeked its head up
out through mulch and tarp
after we dug in autumn
until we saw no more roots.
resilient and determined
i stretch for home with my fingertips.
barely scratch at it with nails
caked in dirt and purslane parts,
shift vertebrae to find comfort
in temporary body, careful not to startle
the earthworms below. i lay down and listen.
listen for my roots, buried so deep,
i will forget this is home until next spring.

how to love a human with an e.d.

one
when her boyfriend decides
they should see other people
ask before you buy fifty dollars' worth
of sour gummy worms and whatchamacallit bars
for a night of binge-eating and rom-coms.
she will say yes, but ask anyway.

two
avoid the bug-eyed stare
when you eat out at olive garden
and the only way she can through the soup,
salad,
and breadsticks
is by dripping sparkling red moon sand through fingers
and coloring caricatures of you.

three
when cuddling beneath the clock tower moon
try your hardest not to graze your fingers
where her shirt rides up
and her pants don't seem to meet.

four
trust
when she says she has to use the restroom after dinner,
with every bone in your body believe
she will keep her meal down
and then casually mention that you also have to pee.

five

do not see her in every eye drowning in dark circles,
each jutting, pale bone,
in picked over and played with salads.
symptoms appear every brain's whisper.

six

laugh.
laugh about eating goddamn bananas
while she's hooked up to potassium iv bags.
keep laughing as the doctor hands her a list
of food to eat and discharges her.
do not think about teenage heart failure
about the fear that froze her fingers
before she finished dialing your number.

seven

console
one in seven die of an eating disorder
and she's already lost two treatment friends
to feeding tubes and ambulance blares.
her funeral dresses have become too loose.

eight

when she falls
and as much as you pray to the god you don't believe in,
she will fall.
stick your hand out to help her up
if she is too weak to grab hold
just lie with her on the bathroom floor.

jean

she chain smoked cigarettes in the kitchen
leaving burn holes in the tablecloth,
leaving butts in the ashtray stained with lipstick.
her own type of rose garden.
told me i better not get pregnant
before i knew about sex.
let me stay up late while we watched nick at night reruns,
said she remembered her tears when the huxtable family
smiled on her tv set.
She fed me apple butter and orange chocolate.
pulled me out of second grade gym class
to get my first relaxer
and as my scalp burned she strongly suggested
that i find and marry a nice catholic man.
displayed my young short stories on her fridge
with alphabet magnets.
told me to try my best. be the best
damn garbage man,
best at wherever my dreams took me.
called me beautiful before a middle school dance.
she took in the neighbor boys to nurse scraped knees
and invited them to stay for dinner,
pork chops and applesauce, always.
snuck cold hands on neck just to watch us jump.
she followed laughter like sunflowers.
blamed her sass on our ancestors,
she was full of pirate's blood.
told me i was powerful,
because my veins pumped with it too.
told me i was sara bernhart, macy gray, lauryn hill.

we watched obama's inauguration together,
lying in bed her teary floorboard voice cracked
said *we did it.*
said *i don't run unless a bear is chasing me.*
said *i can dress myself.*
said *i ain't dead yet.*
said *i am not ready.*
left roses on my cheek,
said *peace be with you too.*
said the optimistic goodbye,
said *i will see you when i see you.*

coffeegrounds

and somewhere between crosswords and coffeegrounds
i manifested sadness as anger,
until i do not know why i am crying,
can't stop.
something about the way orange leaves reflect sunshine
on autumn afternoons.
like i saw her sunday, smiling
and today the tuba tones have left her toes.
left me staring into empty,
trying to recollect the number of books
on my shelf with my grandmother's handwriting
i can't
can't
can't remember
anything, but flashbacks
triggered by creaking doors,
crunching leaves.
remember everything,
took a twenty two hour greyhound
home only to leave
with a taste of stale chips
in my teeth and
espresso beneath my fingernails.
only to come back
to a rusty bicycle in a storm
still, the wheels keep spinning round.
and fall will come next year again.

hairy legs

and i stopped shaving my legs when they weren't smooth
like the other girls with porcelain skin and straight b report cards.
i would come to school and hear the mocking of the off-white dyke oreo
and he once told me no one would ever love a girl like that, like me.
but i filed that away in a cabinet of opinions that used to matter,
because on summer days
in short shorts and tank tops
the cool breeze whispers through my body hair
and reminds me of first kiss tingles
on basement couches with reruns of full house in the background,
reminds me that i love myself.
something that is easy to forget
like where i put my keys
or which theories weber wrote versus marx.
i guess i just got tired of cactus love and wine-stained smiles,
tired of counting ceiling tiles
wondering if i will ever be glamour magazine cover material.
truth is, i will not
nor will you,
but my unphotoshopped stretch marks are lightning strikes
and scars are stories that were not funny at the time,
but my now repeat in my mind with a musical soundtrack of laughter.
inch by inch i will trace my fingers over my textured love body
like braille for i am so sorry for what i have done,
but today is an understatement for good.
my sunburn scabs bow to my fortune cookie, marijuana wisdom
and the wind picks up, cools off,
until i understand what grass blades feel like.
and this, my hair,
is just a pie slice of identity,
but fuck this diet,
piece by piece i will learn to love myself.

calling in black

i am calling in black today,
calling in woman.
last sunday's daylight savings
has made it dark by dinner
and as the chill hits my cheek
i confuse shadow with self
and the ominous other.
allow fear to creep up my fingertips,
too tense to continue on a simple walk
to the corner store.
wishing this was different
than last week,
last year.

i am calling in black today,
calling in woman.
exhausted from coworkers explaining
their new found belief in the reality of racism
after seeing a textbook definition
in the grocery store,
said nothing,
did nothing,
except remind me that my body
is inherently thug,
unceasingly slut
and even a humble existence is a fight for resistance.

i am calling in black today,
calling in woman,
calling in conflicted by being,
breathing, wishing it was as simple,
instead of gradient shaded system of disdain.
speaking well,
for a black girl,
creates an ingrained untaught thought
to hate our roots,
our nose,
our slang.

i am calling in black today,
calling in woman,
audre lorde speaks of the innate necessity
to love oneself
as radical. on my day off
i will perform the radical miracle of survival.

soon after my plea the receiver goes silent,
followed by a breathy laugh from my boss
who informs me *you need to get your ass to work*

woman

daughters of the full moon
eyes reflecting its wonder
blinded be the great i am
lost when it wanes to devious smiles
and then nothing
dizzy from the circling sky
until we find cassiopeia
and her unrivaled beauty
feel grounded by the grass of gaia
between our toes

with lungs full of sweaty summer
air she said
i never really thought i'd be a grown woman
thought i'd be like the men
who surrounded the kitchen table
at family holidays
thought i would be monster
die young
anything but woman

but here we are
like molly ringwald in the eighties
constantly coming of age
discovering epiphanies
of purpose for these tears
this body.
place calloused hands
in each other's palms
unaware of next step
but ready for the exploration
of am.
of woman.

there is no address for a highway ditch

i loved you selfish.
angry my hands were not strong enough
to hold you,
cracking, crumbling,
i felt you slipping
off my hip, babe,
to old, still clinging
tighter.
afraid to lose
what was never mine.
crave you,
the warmth your hand
left on my cheek.
if only our broken bodies
could be bound
without cracking.

hands

i am amazed by strength i never knew i had,
i always thought i could be a super hero if i tried.
strength of who watches the watchman,
who plays into the power,
as i push man against bar wall
before introductions,
in awe of what these hands can do
flattened out,
in fists,
or wrung around neck.
shaking as apology.
and when i learned you were a rapist,
when i saw her crying and emaciated.
rewind. underfed and sobbing on your shoulder,
me, i thought friend
i thought no,
i thought boys will be boys
and girls will be girls
i thought of the strength
of my own hands,
of his,
of hers,
of yours
clandestinely creeping up the freudian conscious.

my lover's bedroom

my bedroom sheets reek of lavender.
pillows and clothes all laced
with scents of home and you
sit there like laughing lemonade,
too much sugar to be bitter. sweet,
like lips and lungs,
your air, breathless.
breathe in the elusive everything;
temporary whispers of happiness
in wrapped honest arms around me
like good morning
stay as long as you would like.

bar close

and the words trip out my mouth,
fall to linoleum, before i can catch them.
she is my bar close kiss. always.
nothing more. before i dangle
off his arm like fringe dancing
as he smiles in my direction.
my eyes watch his lips
call me beautiful
or music fool
my blood has too tainted with
tequila to tell the difference,
to find truth i will ask
if he loves me
and when he hesitates
i will bring up his ex
he will call me drunk,
and when the doctor asks me how much pain i feel.
on a scale of one to ten.
i will say nine and a half
even though bruised lungs breathe different.
and when he hesitates.
i will call him insecure,
possibly projecting.
he will suggest i go to urgent care
about my potential broken rib.
i will suggest that he stops lying about his feelings.
and he will peel me off of his arm slow.
like band-aid, like pain
like even when it stings, leaves skin red
we will ignore tonight
to surround ourselves with cokeheads
who dance like y2k.
after all this only a nine and a half,
and with ibuprofen and a glass of water
we will make a full recovery.

easy sunday morning

we sit on gaudy floral couch
exchange poetry.
fill each other's lungs with angelou and cohen.
let goosebumps touch as we discuss
the social implications
of hooks and the black panther party.
laugh about marx
thank god for bourdieu
somewhere in this field
our social capital cross paths
a happenstance hello
that lead to sunday morning smiles
hungover, hungry to know more
let your lips meet mine,
kiss in iambic pentameter
let rhythm take body in moment
an honest sonnet
of hedonistic joy
flows like river
with a sunset horizon goodbye
until happenstance happens again.

jesus

your jesus was a black man
murdered as the crowd cheered,
just politics,
hung between cigarillo thieves
crying *father, father,*
why have you forsaken me?
my god, my god, i cannot breathe
but at least our sins are cleansed
our officers acquitted.
it is finished.

molotov cocktail

he mistakes her for a glass of white wine,

easy, for a summer evening,

but her smirk grows into a molotov cocktail smile

says she does not shave her armpits

as a warning to prospective lovers,

unable to grasp the infinite of her hips

swinging, though he tries, they try,

but at close she leaves them all behind,

standing on sticky bar floor

jaws unhinged, unable to move,

they are common houseflies,

a constant buzzing distraction

easily caught on a summer evening

while she has revolution in her veins.

uprise

malcolm's anger never quelled,
must be rolling in his grave.
the nine inch knife was only taken out three inches
slowly edged back in
as the reoccurring nightmare
of the sound of soft skin on pavement echoes.
we gather, we march, we mourn
we are called niggers until our names
are turned into hashtags,
thugs until propaganda.
i can write the same poem over and over
just change the name
still relevant
still dying.

martin must be mad,
like raise his voice, pissed off mad.
he marched in washington, selma and chicago
trying to prove that black lives matter,
before they turn blue.
because emmitt till and tamir rice are just kids—
were just kids.
history repeating. strange fruit
skipping on the record player
sandra bland knew the melody,
but breonna taylor was caught off guard by the beat
we may pull up the statues,
but miss the roots
it grows,
grows like roses that bloom
in chests of young black boys
and thorns that choked george floyd
as he cried for his mother

my soul, far from rested,
still says prayers
for the three hundred nigerian girls who disappeared
behind the name of boko haram
and we forgot.
there is no time to rest
when you can feel mother earth hyperventilate.
we may shake, fall
but uprising is survival,
uprising is cursing god and thanking her
with the same breath
it's a funeral had in the motherland,
in new orleans,
in ferguson,
where we dance
and sing
and cry
and riot
the voice of the unheard,
rising from king,
x,
shakur,
seale,
tubman,
and turner.
the phoenix gains strength from
ashes
and we have been burned
for generations,
but refuse silence.

wise women

the women in the kitchen

add laugh lines to show age,

tell me *just you wait*,

as they discuss diabetes and denture care

and cackle about chiropractors.

i stretch to crack bones,

pop body back into place.

they stare in awe

and say *oh honey just you wait*

for earfuls of earwax

and peculiar podiatrist appointments.

and with a wise whisper they leave,

it'll happen to you too.

in the after

we lie in flaws
in childhood scars
in shadows we have yet to illuminate
whisper laughter like secrets
sniffle honesty back into my lungs
but the words lose control
travel to the tip of my tongue
stumble out these lips
resound in her ears.
i can feel the tickle of a tear on my nose
before it hits the pillow
her eyes ask why
i tell her
i am thinking about death,
mourning yesterday,
and all of times before
i felt her breath on my neck.
this tear drying on my cheek
was created from the feeling safety in her sweat
and because the bruises of my body
have found a tender home.
tell her i am thinking
of continuous grieving
for future's uncertainty
and the past's permanence,
of the exhausted content in arms that do not suffocate.
and the rising sun ingrained in her lips.

how to be beautiful

undress yourself in front of the mirror,

gaze at every nook and cranny of your body,

look in awe at the rolls, the bones, the stretch marks.

stare into your own eyes

allow your lips to say *beautiful.*

the words will cut your tongue like glass,

but let it be cut by truth,

let it sting like growing pangs

and then say it again,

until your tongue is raw.

i am beautiful.

reclaim beautiful as mantra.

when you wake up with a scratchy throat

and a new pimple on your nose

i am beautiful.

before you put your makeup on

i am beautiful.

after you are contoured and cat-eyed

i am beautiful.

when you notice your pants fit a little tighter than last time

i am beautiful.

when you keep digging at scabs that should have healed by now

bleeding sore and red

i am beautiful.

every day,

more than once a day,

in the middle of your meal

when they offer you dessert

i am beautiful.

when you are lying in bed

too afraid of nightmares to fall sleep,

say it like you are counting sheep

i am beautiful.

        i am beautiful.

                i am beautiful.

until it is ingrained in your scars,

until you no longer have to convince yourself.

then say it again

i

am

beautiful

but you

i wonder where i should put my hands
front porch swinging singing moldy peaches
running out of fingers and toes to count the number of times
i have watched your lips,

                        wanted them against mine.
i am in love with the idea of you
and i in indie movies
no one understands the plot,
but we get to make out a lot.
swing dancing with tuba tones in our toes,
pass the salt, please,
goose bumps rising from fingertips touching,
and my mind rewinds to summer beach days and winter bonfires,
as you blush,
followed by me,
and i belch,
you laugh,
place your hands on my hips,
let them linger a little longer than last time.
and i don't see what anyone can see in anyone else,

                                  but you.

tights

we've got runs in our tights
because we like the way they look.
like the way they talk, runs say,
yeah, i've seen hell,
scraped my knees crawling out
and the only thing keeping me together
is pitch black nail polish.
they say,
i'm ironically cool
and a little trashy.
i'm gonna strut that shit.

wise for her age

two year old dances,

sings her abcs,

sings woody guthrie,

tells me she is going to the redwood forest,

but just runs circles in our living room.

two year old walks by church

and recollects baptism

tells me she hit the priest. she did.

two year old finds joy in the little things

like mooning us at the breakfast table,

hums dammit while sitting on time out.

two year old screams and kicks

and when i tell her to use her words,

she calms down, tells me she is frustrated

because she just wants a cookie

then tells me she needs to cut down on sugar.

two year old asks for a sip, non a gulp, of my drink

with a please and thank you,

but i tell her no because it is alcohol

and two year old reminds me

that i am drinking poison

and if i have too much i will get sick and die.

two year old runs behind the counter

to give me a hug at work,

yells at me to get out of her house

when she is standing in my room.

she apologizes when i tell her of hurt feelings.

two year old softly sings that *by the relief office*
i seen my people, knows the panhandler
on the highway by name.
two year old cuddles on the couch
as we read piggy and gerald books,
holds her ear, whispers sleepy rambles.
two year old holds my hand tells me i look sad,
tells me she gets sad too,
her matter of fact voice announces
that sometimes she cries to make herself feel better,
and maybe i should try to cry.

christina

this year i remembered

because i had to clock into work on paper.

wrote the date out slow and breathed your name,

forgot how familiar february is

how the sun shone that day,

the brain remembers

moments

not linear

like i waited for you come home,

started hearing the click of the back door in my sleep,

like how i came home craving the indents of my bed

but it didn't hug me like before

the smell of sage and moratorium lingered on,

like i wanted to tell you i failed my driver's test.

cried during the ninety degree back in,

and you would have laughed.

it always raised your spirits when my human showed,

but when i knocked on your door

all i heard were the sharp knives of silence,

like i settled for an air mattress

surrounded by middle school knick knacks

all night i would count the shag rug loops,

hoping they would lull me to sleep,

just learned i could count real high,

like the last time i saw you

i didn't see you,

i saw potential mice

around littered ice cream containers,

i thought name your sad and carry on.

apathetic burn out eking from my pores,

like we planted gladiolas for you,

set bulbs in the rainy earth with your mother

who had stories, heard stories.

laughed

like you.

like the deflating air mattress was stepped on

by my friend's kid at three in the morning,

i cannot sleep, i need my mom

came from her sleepy voice

two hundred thirty eight, two hundred thirty nine,

two hundred forty, your mom is sleeping,

we were in temporary together

she said, *micholle*, her little voice cracking

i cannot sleep, i need a hug

so held on until she cried

a sadness without a name,

until she fell asleep,

like i should've held you.

privilege

the woman at the bar sips her pbr
asks her friends if she should get arrested tomorrow
as if it is a choice,
isn't it?
to stand with a toe over the trespassing line,
dance on hot pavement during six a.m. traffic
asking for attention,
but not for self.
laughter of her friends fills the room
as they tell stories of
their own arrest records.
smile about the highways
and pipe yards. the stories go quiet
as they arrive to the jail.
remember truth of feeling
less than in core
to have privilege stripped off,
placed in booking.
given back.
remember that others lost bragging rights
centuries before they are born
the women at the bar sips their pbr
asks her friends if she should get arrested tomorrow
as if it is a choice.

phased

i choose to leave the last chapter unread,
an open invitation to come back home,
an infinite forever instead of goodbye.
keep a blank or two unanswered in a monday crossword
in case of rainy days where i need a win,
need to feel accomplished all the way down to my fingertips
and i end poems with the possibility you will crave me again,

i miss you and

unapologetic *

*sorry.

suddenly embarrassed of all things feminine

like breasts

and emotions

and a shedding uterine wall.

learning parts of me i never knew to be ashamed of before,

like nicks on legs

from shaving in the fifth grade

blood circling the drain.

*sorry

but we all bleed beets and cry when onions are cut.

as i start to tear up over spilled milk

i tell her i am menstruating

even when i am not

something about being a woman.

something about unapologetic epiphanies

stuck in the back of my throat. never said.

*sorry

for existing,

taking up space.

*sorry

for body,

for movement.

i scrub sheets with vinegar,

rubbing alcohol

and a toothbrush too old for teeth.

something about being a woman

unable to get a handle,

shattering ceramics keep breaking,

scrubbing clockwise

like clock work

every month,

since middle school,

minus a pregnancy scare or two.

*sorry

like déjà vu

like salt on cutting boards

with beet juice

until next month's borscht.

do you pray?

snorted on the jags of apartment key
she can feel the energy of living
hitchhiking on veins
and yet
she continues to think
of how earlier today her sage
looked kissed by death
but rain, like miracle
revived.
she continues to think
of the humans she saw
grasp for life
in drought.
i watch her run into the middle of the road
and scream at the sky
goddammit
      goddammit
            goddammit.

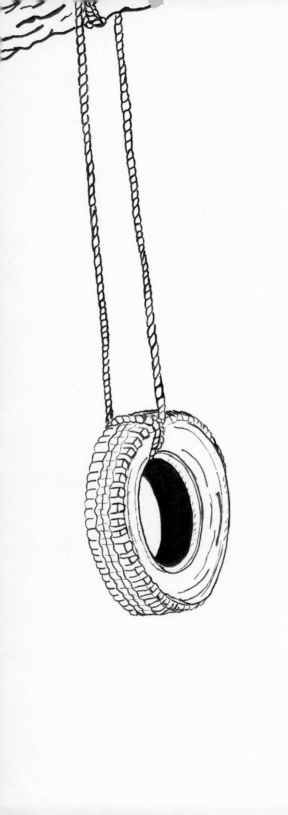

nothing more

maybe you and i will be nothing more
than a night,
no more than a brief whisper of magnolias,
or a sunburnt summer playing
bags on the beach.
maybe we will break
at a wrong turn roaming road trip
or an all night fight
we label as conversation,
until one of us,
probably me, humbles themselves
to say sorry.
maybe we'll create nothing more
than a crisp ironed shirt
a skirt made for celebration,
nothing more than
a backyard full of black-eyed
susans and a tire swing
nothing more than tradition,
than a hopeful wishbone break
of tomorrow.

stories

part one

> my father used to tell me stories,
> pour me a cold can of pepsi
> and speak of his youth.
> i would hang on to every word.
> stories of parties conquered and curfew broken
> of why he doesn't listen to the doors anymore.
> he had stories about the price of inflation in germany.
> and how he used to drink beer in the back of pick ups
> on senior skip days.
> but before some stories he would get real quiet,
> turn down the ever-playing npr
> and say, nickie, the world has always been a cruel place

part two

> he would tell me stories of cars that saw him in the crosswalk
> and only added a little pressure to the gas pedal.
> stores he and my uncles were kicked out of for loitering
> while his white friends continued to peruse the chip aisle.
> my father cried when zimmerman was acquitted.
> recounts the time a short kwik trip visit ended
> with an officer pointing a gun to his head.
> said nigger was the nicest word they called him
> as a crowd of his neighbors watched, said nothing.
> reminds me to stay safe. tells me in the north
> i can get as big as i want,
> but do not get any closer.

part three

    we call, sit in silence,

    as if memorial for all the black lives lost since we last talked

    say we do not understand, but cannot be surprised

    cause we have heard the stories:

    like kinsey lying on a basketball court

    with his hands up, begging not to be shot.

    like the irony too thick in garner's last words.

    like the uncanny resemblance between trayvon

    and my cousin khalid.

    we try to keep these stories light so before we hang up

    my father jokes about the hand gun on his hip.

    says you've seen what they do to unarmed black men in this country.

part four

    as soon as we heard the news, the latest story:

    philando shot point-blank range. his last words

    streamed live on facebook

    i was not reaching for it. i wasn't reaching my gun

    my father and held memorial for longer than before.

    unsure how to comfort, how to cope.

    no jokes, no silence.

    i told him not to carry his gun in his car anymore

    and he told me to stop standing on highways.

    a little more scared than last time

    we say be safe, but wonder if it's possible.

    we have heard too many stories

bug bites

swollen bug bites are totally worth it
for late nights between tiny mountains
with bratwursts and ipas
where i keep on catching glimpses
of you catching glimpses of me.
could go on as if everything were perfectly fine,
but what you said last week contradicts
the way you blush each time i enter a room.
look at me as if your eyes are peeking
behind hide-and-go-seek hands
                                        i'm right fucking here.
laughing too loud at bad puns.
forgetting how to frown
when i catch your lingering eyes.

on a scale from friends to i want to bone you
i don't know where i stand,
but i know where i'd like to be
because the next day at in art class
i am scratching my bug-bitten ass
with a dorky grin on my face
mentioning your name
in conversations that have nothing
to do with you. your name is constantly on my lips.
it would be nice if you were too.

illustrations

Cover Art: Ejiwa "Edge" Ebenebe
Edge explores whimsical worlds and ethereal, opulent
figures, aiming to help increase positive representations
of Black people in fantasy art.
See her work at www.artofedge.com

Interior Art: Lukas Ramsey
Lukas Ramsey is an artist and writer based out of the
Twin Cities in Minnesota. In his free time he performs
stand-up comedy and makes 'zines.
See his work at www.ramseycreation.com

acknowledgments

Thank you.
This could not have been done without these wonderful beings:

Teresa Barnes

Dawne & Bill Carlson

Bill Hazell

G'ma Hazell

Keaton Hazell

Mary Hazell

Tucker Hazell

Anthony Laurnoff

Jess & Ryan Loesel

Ken McCullough

Phoenix ❤

The Raben Family

Jerome Ramsey

MaMa Ramsey & her Boys

Carole & Alan Sincic

Matt Sincic

Mary Ann & Tom Shurtleff

Rejina & Ryan Sincic

Steve & Denise Sincic

Tom & Sally Sincic

Tony & Joanie Sincic

The Sincic Family, Los Angeles

Rachael Storey

Sydney Swanson

Sarah Taubner

The Anonymous Angels

the team

Pat Hazell at Sweetwood Creative

Brian McDonald at Talking Drum LLC

Lisa Pelto & Ellie Godwin at Concierge Publishing Services

about the author

nicholle ramsey is a confessional poet from the Midwest. She held the title of Associate Poet Laureate of Winona, Minnesota, from 2017-2018. She is known in the driftless region for her spoken word performances and incredibly loud laugh. She currently resides in Eagle River, Alaska, for insight and inspiration. *calling in black* is her first published collection.

sometimes, published in *Folk Opera* 2018
how to love a human with an e.d., published in *Soundings* 2015
hairy legs, published in *Mother Earth News* 2016